MASIAKASAURUS

and Other Fish-Eating Dinosaurs

by **Dougal Dixon**

illustrated by **Steve Weston and James Field**

PICTURE WINDOW BOOKS
Minneapolis, Minnesota

Picture Window Books
151 Good Counsel Drive
P.O. Box 669
Mankato, MN 56002-0669
877-845-8392
www.picturewindowbooks.com

Printed in the United States of America.

All books published by Picture Window Books
are manufactured with paper containing at
least 10 percent post-consumer waste.

Library of Congress Cataloging-in-Publication Data
Dixon, Dougal.
Masiakasaurus and other fish-eating dinosaurs /
by Dougal Dixon ; illustrated by Steve Weston and
James Field.
p. cm. — (Dinosaur find)
Includes index.
ISBN 978-1-4048-5171-9 (library binding)
1. Dinosaurs—Juvenile literature. 2. Dinosaurs—
Food—Juvenile literature. I. Weston, Steve, ill. II. Field,
James, 1959- ill. III. Title.
QE861.5.D599 2009
567.912—dc22   2008043406

Acknowledgments
This book was produced for Picture Window Books
by Bender Richardson White, U.K.

Illustrations by James Field (cover and pages 4–5, 7,
11, 15, 21) and Steve Weston (pages 9, 13, 17, 19).
Diagrams by Stefan Chabluk.

Photographs: Frank Lane Picture Agency page 16
(Rob Reijnen/Foto Natura/FLPA), iStockphoto
pages 6 (Johan Swanepoel), 8 (David Hutchison),
10, 12 (Michael Willis), 14 (John Pitcher), 18, 20
(Igor Karon).

Consultant: John Stidworthy, Scientific Fellow of
the Zoological Society, London, and former
Lecturer in the Education Department, Natural
History Museum, London.

Types of dinosaurs

In Dinosaur Find books,
a red shape at the top of a
left-hand page shows the
animal was a meat-eater.
A green shape shows it was
a plant-eater.

Just how big—or small—were they?

Dinosaurs were many different
sizes. We have compared their
size to one of the following:

Chicken
2 feet (60 centimeters) tall
Weight 6 pounds (2.7 kilograms)

Adult person
6 feet (1.8 meters) tall
Weight 170 pounds (76.5 kg)

Elephant
10 feet (3 m) tall
Weight 12,000 pounds
(5,400 kg)

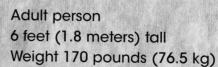

TABLE OF CONTENTS

WHAT'S INSIDE?

Dinosaurs! These dinosaurs lived and hunted between 230 million and 65 million years ago. Find out how they lived and what they have in common with today's animals.

LIFE AS A FISH-EATER

Dinosaurs lived between 230 million and 65 million years ago. The world did not look the same then. Much of the land and many of the seas were not in the same places as today. But there were plenty of lakes and rivers full of fish, and there were dinosaurs that hunted the fish.

At the edge of a lake, small dinosaurs such as *Pelecanimimus* and *Huaxiagnathus* looked for an easy meal. The bigger *Baryonyx* waded in the shallow water. All of these dinosaurs ate any fish they could easily catch.

BARYONYX

Pronunciation:
BAR-ee-ON-ix

Baryonyx waded through the mud and clumps of water plants looking for food. There were lots of fish to find in the swamps and plant beds. *Baryonyx* pounced on anything that moved in the water.

Swamp fishers today

With their long legs and bills, storks hunt fish in the shallow water, just like *Baryonyx* once did.

Size Comparison

When *Baryonyx* saw a fish in the shallow water, it darted at the fish with its long jaws and sharp little teeth.

Spinosaurus was one of the biggest meat-eating dinosaurs. It had a sail on its back that it used to signal to other animals. *Spinosaurus* lived near water and sometimes caught fish. It also lived near desert oases.

Big eaters today

The modern black bear needs lots of food to keep its big body going. It eats many different kinds of animals, just like *Spinosaurus* once did.

Size Comparison

Spinosaurus ate all sorts of things. It ate fish, dead dinosaurs, and even pterosaurs as they landed on the ground.

MASIAKASAURUS

Pronunciation:
MAS-ee-ah-ka-SAW-rus

An animal that eats fish needs special teeth. *Masiakasaurus* had long, thin, pointed teeth at the front of its mouth. With these teeth, it grabbed fish as it hunted on riverbanks in what is now Madagascar.

Fish hunters today

The modern gavial crocodile uses pointy teeth to catch fish, just like *Masiakasaurus* did long ago.

Size Comparison

10

Once *Masiakasaurus* caught a fish, the fish struggled and twisted to get away. But it could not escape. *Masiakasaurus* simply swallowed the fish whole.

11

Poikilopleuron lived along shorelines. It scavenged among the waste washed up by the tides. Among the seashells, seaweed, and driftwood there would have been dead fish and other sea creatures. *Poikilopleuron* would have eaten some of these dead animals.

Shoreline scavengers today

Modern seagulls peck at the garbage that washes up on beaches. Like *Poikilopleuron* once did, the seagulls eat the dead things they find.

Size Comparison

The smell of dead fish attracted *Poikilopleuron*. The dinosaur would have loved eating a big fish.

HUAXIAGNATHUS

Pronunciation: HUA-shi-GNAY-thus

Huaxiagnathus was a small meat-eating dinosaur that lived beside lakes in what is now China. It ran through the low-lying plants. *Huaxiagnathus* ate all kinds of things, including any fish it could catch.

Fish-eating animals today

Modern wolves are fish-eating animals, just like *Huaxiagnathus* once was.

Size Comparison

14

If a fish came too close to the shore of the lake, *Huaxiagnathus* would have snapped it up.

IRRITATOR

Pronunciation:
EER-ee-TAY-tor

Irritator was a fish-eating dinosaur similar to *Baryonyx* and *Spinosaurus*. It had to hunt all day to catch enough fish to keep itself and its family alive. *Irritator* built its nest close to water.

Feeding animals today

Many birds swallow fish and fly back to their nests. Then the birds spit up the fish back into their mouths to feed to their young, hungry chicks.

Size Comparison

At its nest, *Irritator* spit up the fish it had already swallowed. It fed the fish to its youngsters.

SUCHOMIMUS

Pronunciation:
SOO-cho-MYE-mus

Suchomimus sometimes hunted for fish along the shoreline. But hunting was a dangerous task. *Suchomimus* had to watch out for *Sarcosuchus,* a large crocodile that lived in the water. The crocodile would have been able to kill big fish-eating dinosaurs like *Suchomimus.*

Hunters in danger today

Modern lake-living birds have to watch out for crocodiles and other water hunters, just as *Suchomimus* once did.

Size Comparison

While *Suchomimus* looked for fish, *Sarcosuchus* jumped up from the water to grab its next meal.

PELECANIMIMUS

Pelecanimimus was a small dinosaur that had a pouch under its chin. It lived along the banks of lakes in what is now Spain. *Pelecanimimus* hunted for fish in shallow waters.

Pouched beaks today

The modern pelican has a pouch as the lower part of its beak. The bird uses the pouch to scoop up fish from the water, as *Pelecanimimus* did long ago.

Size Comparison

20

Pelecanimimus collected fish and other food in its pouch to feed its family.

21

WHERE DID THEY GO?

Dinosaurs are extinct, which means that none of them are alive today. Scientists study rocks and fossils to find clues about what happened to dinosaurs.

People have different explanations about what happened. Some people think a huge asteroid that hit Earth caused all sorts of climate changes, which caused the dinosaurs to die. Others think volcanic eruptions caused the climate change and that killed the dinosaurs. No one knows for sure what happened to all of the dinosaurs.

GLOSSARY

beak—the hard front part of the mouth of birds and some dinosaurs; also known as a bill

oases—places in the desert where there is water, often in pools

pterosaurs—flying animals that lived at the same time as some dinosaurs

sail—a tall, thin upright structure on the back of some animals

scavenge—to feed on the bodies of animals that are already dead

signal—to make a sign, warning, or hint

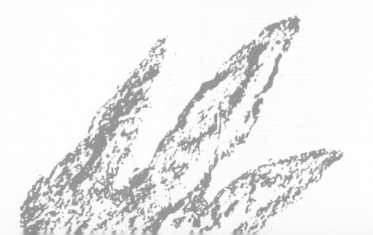

To Learn More

More Books to Read

Clark, Neil, and William Lindsay. *1001 Facts About Dinosaurs.* New York: Dorling Kindersley, 2002.

Dixon, Dougal. *Dougal Dixon's Amazing Dinosaurs.* Honesdale, Penn.: Boyds Mills Press, 2007.

Holtz, Thomas R., and Michael Brett-Surman. *Jurassic Park Institute Dinosaur Field Guide.* New York: Random House, 2001.

On the Web

FactHound offers a safe, fun way to find educator-approved Internet sites related to this book.

Here's what you do:
1. Visit *www.facthound.com*
2. Choose your grade level.
3. Begin your search.

This book's ID number is 9781404851719

Index

Look for other books in the Dinosaur Find series: